The Teaching Research
Motor-Development Scale

The Teaching Research Motor-Development Scale

For
Moderately and Severely Retarded Children

By

H. D. BUD FREDERICKS
VICTOR L. BALDWIN
PHILIP DOUGHTY
L. JAMES WALTER

Illustrated by
Wendy Fredericks

Photographs by
Teaching Research Photographic Staff
Teaching Research Division
Oregon State System of Higher Education
Monmouth, Oregon

CHARLES C THOMAS · PUBLISHER
Springfield · Illinois · U.S.A.

Published and Distributed Throughout the World by

CHARLES C THOMAS • PUBLISHER

BANNERSTONE HOUSE

301-327 East Lawrence Avenue, Springfield, Illinois, U.S.A.

NATCHEZ PLANTATION HOUSE

735 North Atlantic Boulevard, Fort Lauderdale, Florida, U.S.A.

This book is protected by copyright. No part of it may be reproduced in any manner without written permission from the publisher.

© *1972, by* CHARLES C THOMAS • PUBLISHER

ISBN 0-398-02284-4

Library of Congress Catalog Card Number: 79-161158

With THOMAS BOOKS *careful attention is given to all details of manufacturing and design. It is the Publisher's desire to present books that are satisfactory as to their physical qualities and artistic possibilities and appropriate for their particular use.* THOMAS BOOKS *will be true to those laws of quality that assure a good name and good will.*

Printed in the United States of America

H-13

362.3
T22

APPL. LIFE STUDIES

To the teachers in the State of Oregon who spent many hours administering variations of this scale and to their retarded students from whom we are always learning.

INTRODUCTION

General Purpose

The purpose of this scale is to measure motor proficiency. It does not purport to measure general intelligence, nor does it infer any relationship between intelligence scales and motor proficiency. The scale is designed to be used by teachers of the moderately and severely retarded either in the classroom or in physical education programs. The scale provides a vehicle for determining the capabilities of a child in various motor proficiency areas. It can be used also as a model for a teaching curriculum to improve motor proficiency and motor coordination among the severely and moderately retarded. It has value for researchers who need to determine improved motor performance as a result of an experimental motor research program.

Development and Research

This scale had its beginning in 1968 at Fairview Hospital and Training Center, Salem, Oregon in a motor development research effort with children, aged 7 to 12, with Down's Syndrome. The *Lincoln-Oseretsky Motor Development Scale* (William Sloan, C. H. Stoelting Company, Chicago, Illinois, (1954) was utilized and found to contain items not geared low enough to score the fully developed motor abilities of these handicapped children. Thus, new items were developed to test skills appropriate to this population. In addition, some of the items on the *Lincoln-Oseretsky Motor Development Scale* were revised and simplified so as to allow retarded children to achieve scores. Other items, similar to activities included in most physical education programs, such as arm movements, pull-ups, push-ups, and sit-ups, were added. However, even these needed simplified versions of the standard activity. The basic presentation styles of the *Lincoln-Oseretsky Motor Development Scale* were found to be understandable and highly acceptable to most teachers and researchers. Thus, the same type of format has been maintained in this scale, and the same type of acceptability has been found.

Thus, the test utilizes concepts of testing developed elsewhere and primarily reflected in the *Lincoln-Oseretsky Motor Development Scale*. Since its initial development in 1968, the *Teaching Research Motor Development Scale* has been used on a series of populations, both institutionalized and community based, and varying in age from pre-school to high school.

Although this scale can certainly be used with children less retarded than those categorized as moderately or severely retarded, the motor proficiency of these less handicapped children can probably best be measured by a scale such as the *Lincoln-Oseretsky Motor Development Scale*. Over five hundred children have been tested utilizing the scale, so that it has now been modified to the point where severely and moderately retarded children in a preschool setting are able to achieve scores; yet the scale still does not have too low a ceiling for those in the severely and moderately retarded range who may possess more advanced motor skills or who are older. Therefore, the test discriminates both at the preschool level and high school level for the severely and moderately retarded.

Norms

No norms are assigned to this scale because of the nature of the population for which it is designed. Norms must depend upon either a chronological age or mental age. Since children in the severely and moderately retarded range exhibit wide variations of combinations of these two measurements, norming is considered neither possible nor essential. Each child must be treated as an individual and his performance on the scale must be measured against his future performance or past performance, or against some arbitrary standards which the examiner or teacher prescribes.

ADMINISTRATION AND SCORING

General Instructions

Throughout this scale the symbol "C" means child and "E" means examiner. The test is divided into parts which may be administered separately. Thus, a teacher or researcher may use the entire test or selected parts of the test.

Directions

This scale is designed to measure motor proficiency and not intelligence. The examiner must make every effort to insure that the retarded child understands what is expected of him. Verbal directions in many cases may have to be minimized. Demonstrations by the examiner should be used extensively if necessary. To insure understanding with some of the more severely retarded children it may be necessary for the examiner to initially guide the child's hands and feet through the task. The important thing to determine with this scale is whether or not the child can do the task. Regardless of the amount of preliminary instruction necessary, if the child can eventually demonstrate that he can accomplish this task, his performance should be scored as a success.

Special consideration should be given by the examiner to insure a suitable visual contrast between the item(s) or equipment used in the test and the background. Suggested items to be considered include the following:

1. Color of table top
2. Color of floor vs. color of line
3. Color of square target vs. color of wall
4. Color of matchsticks vs. color of table top
5. Color of pennies vs. color of table top
6. Color of rope vs. color of floor
7. Color of rod vs. color of floor

The color and composition of the table top are important variables that need to be considered. A dark background will contrast well with the pennies and a light background will contrast well with the matchsticks. A two-foot square of crease-resistant cloth in a pastel green color should control for composition differences and allow enough contrast for both the pennies and matchsticks.

Other suggestions include consideration of the table height for different sized subjects and different height of the ball target for different sized subjects.

With all motor development activities, fatigue is an important consideration and especially so for the retarded population for which this scale is designed. With younger children, it is recommended that the total scale not be administered during one testing period. With all aged children, adequate rest periods should be allowed periodically. The most valid results have been achieved by administering only one or two lettered sections a day.

Materials and Testing Facilities

The test is capable of being administered in classrooms, although regular physical education facilities are certainly preferable. It has been demonstrated that all items where the child is not sitting at a desk or table and section Q can be administered in a cleared area 10 feet by 10 feet. It is believed that most classrooms can achieve that amount of cleared space by temporarily rearranging classroom furniture.

A table or desk and two straight-back chairs will be needed. Regular student desk and chairs are usually suitable. For all paper and pencil items, it is recommended that the paper be secured to the desk with cellophane tape.

Test materials are listed below. After each item the test number in which the item is used is given.

1. Scoring sheet.
2. Two plastic or wooden boxes, inside dimension 4″ × 4″ × 2″ high—H-2 and H-3.
3. One plastic or wooden box, inside dimension 4″ × 4″ × 5″ high—H-1.
4. Thread on wooden spool. Thread is No. 20 and should be unwound seventy-eight inches. Spool cylinder (on which thread is wound) is 2 ⅜ inches in circumference by 1 ⅛ inches long.

Circumference of outer rim of spool is five inches. Overall length of spool is 2 3/8 inches—I-1 and I-2.

5. Twenty matchsticks two inches long with no more than one-eighth-inch variation from this length. Ordinary "kitchen size" matches with heads removed—H-1, 2 and 3.

6. Wooden target and ball. Target is ten inches square, any thickness, attached to string for hanging on nail—M-3.

7. Regulation tennis ball—M1, 2, 3.

8. Two poles mounted on plywood stands one-foot square with two-inch nails placed on one side of the poles at each six inches of height with one and one-fourth inches of the head side of the nail protruding—C-2.

9. White paper with four sets of two parallel lines each one-half inch between lines, one inch between sets. Size of sheet may vary from 8″ × 10″ to 8½″ × 11″—J-2.

10. Mazes and pencils—J-3.

11. Concentric circles—K-3.

12. Blunt pointed scissors—K-1, 2, and 3.

13. Two pencils and plain white paper. Pencils should not have fine points. Number 2 pencils about five inches long are satisfactory—J-1.

14. Ten pennies—H-3.

15. Four thumbtacks (for holding up target in M-3, holding down paper in J-1, 2, and 3).

16. Tape measure (for measuring distances and marking lines).

17. 6-1′ × 1′ rubber or sponge mats with four-inch diameter painted circle on center of each—D-1 and 2.

18. Chalk, tape, or paint (for marking lines).

19. Four to five foot long broom handle or similar rod—G-1, 2, 3, and 4.

20. Paper strips 8½″ × 3″—K-1.

21. Paper strips 11″ × 6″ with one one-half-inch wide dark line cutting each strip into two 5¼″ × 6″ boxes—K-2.

22. Bar for pull-ups—N-1, N-2, N-3.

23. Five inch rubber ball—L1, 2, 3, 4.

CONTENTS

The Teaching Research
Motor-Development Scale

A

A-1. STANDING ON TIPTOE, EYES OPEN

Equipment: None

Number of Trials: Two (if necessary)

Directions: Stand on toes in an upright position, feet together, eyes open (see Fig. 1).

Scoring Criteria: Success if C stands on toes as described for five seconds without shifting feet, without hopping, and without touching heels to floor.

Points: Success on first or second trial = 3

Failure on first and second trial = 0

Figure 1. Standing on tiptoe, eyes open.

A-2. STANDING ON TIPTOE, EYES CLOSED

Equipment: None

Number of Trials: Two (if necessary)

Directions: Stand on toes in an upright position, feet together, eyes
closed (see Fig. 1, but eyes should be closed).

Scoring Criteria: Success if C remains standing on toes for five seconds without shifting feet, hopping, touching heels to floor,
or opening eyes.

Points: Success on first or second trial = 3
Failure on first and second trial = 0

A-3. CROUCHING ON TIPTOES

Equipment: None

Number of Trials: Two (if necessary)

Directions: C is to stand on tiptoe in a semicrouched position with
knees flexed approximately 45 degrees, and arms extended
horizontally at the sides. Feet are parallel and approximately
one foot apart (see Fig. 2).

Scoring Criteria: Success if C maintains the position for five seconds
without putting weight on heels, touching floor with hands,

Figure 2. Crouching on tiptoes.

or stepping out of place. The arms should be maintained in an essentially straight horizontal position.

Points: Success on first or second trial = 3

Failure on first and second trial = 0

B

B-1. STANDING HEEL TO TOE, EYES OPEN

Equipment: None

Number of Trials: Two (if necessary)

Directions: Stand in an upright position, eyes open with one foot placed directly in front of the other so that the heel of the forward foot touches the toe of the other (see Fig. 3).

Scoring Criteria: Success if C stands heel to toe as directed for five seconds without breaking heel-toe contact between feet.

Points: Success on first or second trial = 3

Failure on first and second trial = 0

B-2. STANDING HEEL TO TOE WITH EYES CLOSED

Equipment: None

Number of Trials: Two (if necessary)

Directions: Stand in an upright position eyes closed, with one foot placed directly in front of the other so that the heel of the

Figure 3. Standing heel to toe.

forward foot touches the toe of the other (see Fig. 3, but eyes should be closed).

Scoring Criteria: Success if C stands heel to toe as directed for five seconds without opening eyes or breaking heel-toe contact between feet.

Points: Success on first or second trial = 3
Failure on first and second trial = 0

B-3. STANDING ON ONE FOOT, EYES OPEN

Equipment: None

Number of Trials: Two (if necessary)

Directions: Stand with full weight of body on one foot only with eyes open. Then repeat using other foot (see Fig. 4).

Scoring Criteria: Success if C is able to stand on one foot as directed for five seconds without touching other foot to floor or without hopping.

Points: Success on first or second trial with right foot = 3
Failure on first and second trial with right foot = 0
Success on first or second trial with left foot = 3
Failure on first and second trial with left foot = 0

Figure 4. Standing on one foot, eyes open.

B-4. STANDING ON ONE FOOT, EYES CLOSED

Equipment: None

Number of Trials: Two (if necessary) for each foot

Directions: Stand with full weight of body on one foot only, with eyes closed. Then repeat using other foot (see Fig. 4, with eyes closed).

Scoring Criteria: Success if C is able to stand on one foot as described for five seconds without touching other foot to floor, without hopping, and without opening eyes.

Points: Success on first or second trial with right foot — 3
Failure on first and second trial with right foot = 0
Success on first or second trial with left foot = 3
Failure on first and second trial with left foot = 0

C

C-1. JUMP ON TOES RAPIDLY

Equipment: None

Number of Trials: Two (if necessary)

Directions: Jump up and down rapidly on toes with feet together (see Fig. 5).

Scoring Criteria: Success if C jumps with feet together up and down on toes and only toes for five times in five seconds or less.

Points: Success on first or second trial = 3

Failure on first and second trial = 0

Figure 5. Jumping on toes rapidly.

C-2. JUMPING A BAR

a. Ankle Height
b. Between Ankle and Knee
c. Knee Height

Equipment: A bar four feet long and two poles mounted on plywood stands, one foot square, with two-inch nails placed on the side of poles at each six inches of height with one and one-fourth inches of the head side of the nail protruding.

Number of Trials: Two per height (if necessary)

Directions: The bar should be mounted on the nails of the two poles to achieve the desired height so that the bar is even with the ankles, between the ankles and knees, or even with the knees. C should jump with both feet together and the knees should flex at the same time as in a standing broad jump. C should jump without the feet touching the bar (see Fig. 6).

Figure 6. Jumping a bar.

Scoring Criteria: Success if C completes each jump keeping feet together without touching the bar.

Points for Each of the Three Heights: Success on first or second trial = 3

Failure on first and second trial = 0

D

D-1. WALKING FORWARD ON A STRAIGHT LINE OF MATS

Equipment: Six one-foot square rubber or sponge mats with four-inch diameter circles painted in the center of each.

Number of Trials: Two (if necessary)

Directions: The mats should be placed in a straight line six inches apart. They may be placed closer together for very small children. Examiner should demonstrate the proper procedure of stepping in the center of each mat with first one foot and then the other foot until all six have been stepped upon. E may have to place child's feet on each mat to give C the idea. E should state that C is not to "go off" the mats during the trial. C is allowed one practice trip after E is convinced the child understands (see Fig. 7).

Figure 7. Walking forward on a straight line of mats.

Scoting Criteria: Success if C is able to step inside each of the six
mats without missing all or part of any mat.

Points: Success on first or second trial = 3

Failure on first and second trial = 0

D-2. WALKING FORWARD ON STAGGERED MATS

Equipment: Six one-foot square rubber or sponge mats with four-inch
diameter circles painted in the center of each

Number of Trials: Two (if necessary)

Directions: The mats should be placed staggered so that the "upper"
right hand corner of one mat touches the lower left hand
corner of the second mat and the upper left hand corner
of the second mat touches the lower right hand corner of
the third mat and so on for a total of six mats. E should
demonstrate the proper procedure of stepping in the center
of each mat making certain that C understands that he is not
to "go off" the mats. C is allowed one practice trip after E
is convinced C understands (see Fig. 8).

Figure 8. Walking forward on staggered mats.

Scoring Criteria: Success if C is able to step inside each mat in one trip without missing all or part of any mat.

Points: Success on first or second trial = 3

Failure on first and second trial = 0

D-3. WALKING FORWARD ON A SIX-FOOT RADIUS SEMICIRCLE

Equipment: A six-foot radius semicircle, one inch wide, in chalk, paint, or tape placed on a smooth floor free from any obstacles.

Number of Trials: Two (if necessary)

Directions: C is to walk normally along the line placing each foot on the line. E should demonstrate the proper procedure and allow C one practice trip after E is convinced C understands (see Fig. 9).

Scoring Criteria: Success if C successfully walks the length of the semicircle without completely missing the line one time with either foot.

Figure 9. Walking forward on a six-foot radius semicircle.

Points: Success on first or second trial = 3

　　　Failure on first and second trial = 0

D-4. WALKING ALONG A SIX-FOOT LINE HEEL TO TOE

Equipment: Straight line on floor six-feet long, one inch wide, in chalk, paint, or tape placed on a smooth floor free from any obstacles.

Number of Trials: Two (if necessary)

Directions: C is to walk along the line placing heel to toe as he steps. E should make certain that C understands that he is to touch heel to toe each time and that he should keep both feet on the line at all times (see Fig. 10).

Scoring Criteria: Success if C is able to walk the length of the line as directed, keeping both feet on it for the entire length and consistently touching the heel of the forward foot to the toe of the other on each step taken.

Points: Success on first or second trial = 3

　　　Failure on first and second trial = 0

Figure 10. Walking along a six-foot line heel to toe.

D-5. WALKING BACKWARDS

Equipment: None

Number of Trials: Two (if necessary)

Directions: C is to walk backwards six feet, heel to toe. With each step, the toe of the moving foot must be placed behind the heel of the stationary foot.

Scoring Criteria: Success if C does not deviate more than one foot in either direction from the line laterally. If C fails to touch heel to toe more than three times, trial is a failure.

Points: Success on first or second trial = 3

Failure on first and second trial = 0

E

E-1. IMITATIONS OF MOVEMENTS

Equipment: None

Number of Trials: Two (if necessary)

Directions: E faces the child standing three to five feet away. Allow enough room so the child can move his arms freely when they are fully extended. The child is asked to imitate or mirror the movement of E's arms. C is allowed to practice following E through the first three moves before beginning the trial. E moves through each of the nine positions *in order* waiting for the C's response at each position (see Fig. 11).

Figure 11. Imitations of movements.

[17]

Scoring Criteria: A trial consists of completing all nine movements. Success if C does not make a false move with one or both arms. C has five seconds to make a correction.

Points: Success on first or second trial = 3

Failure on first and second trial = 0

F

F-1. TOUCHING NOSE

Equipment: None

Number of Trials: Two (if necessary)

Directions: C is to stretch both arms out to the sides horizontally with index fingers extended (see Fig. 12) and then touch his nose with each hand three times in succession. Eyes are kept open and the head is kept still. (see Fig. 13).

Scoring Criteria: Success if C touches the nose twice in the three attempts with each hand.

Points: Success on first or second trial = 3
Failure on first and second trial = 0

Figure 12. Touching nose.

F-2. TOUCHING FINGERTIPS

Equipment: None

[19]

Figure 13. Touching nose.

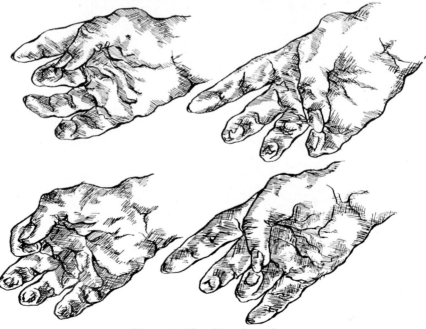

Figure 14. Touching fingertips.

Number of Trials: Two (if necessary) for each hand.

Directions: C is to touch all the fingertips of one hand in succession with the thumb of the same hand beginning with the little finger. (see Fig 14).

Scoring Criteria: There is a ten second time limit for each trial. Success if C does not touch a finger more than once, touch two fingers at the same time with the thumb, or does not skip one or more fingers.

Points: Success on first or second trial for right hand = 3
Failure on first and second trial for right hand = 0
Success on first or second trial for left hand = 3
Failure on first and second trial for left hand = 0

F-3. CLOSE AND OPEN HANDS ALTERNATELY

Equipment: None

Number of Trials: Two (if necessary)

Directions: C is to extend his arms in front of him. C is to close his right hand making a fist, and at a given signal he must open it and close the left one, continuing in this manner as fast as possible for ten seconds (see Fig. 15).

Scoring Criteria: A trial is passed if C does not open and shut his hands at the same time.

Points: Success on first or second trial = 3
Failure on first and second trial = 0

F-4. TAPPING RHYTHMICALLY WITH FEET AND FINGERS

Equipment: None

Number of Trials: Two (if necessary)

Directions: While seated, C is to tap the floor rhythmically with the soles of the feet, performing the movement alternately with each foot at any speed he elects. At the same time, the corresponding index fingers are to tap the table top which is placed in front of C. The finger and foot tapping should be synchronous.

Scoring Criteria: The trial is passed if C maintains the rhythmic tapping for at least fifteen seconds. The trial is failed if the

Figure 15. Close and open hands alternately.

rhythm of the movement is changed, or if the tapping does not correspond to that of the same foot.

Points: Success on first or second trial = 3

Failure on first and second trial = 0

G

G-1. STEPPING OVER A KNEE-HIGH OBSTACLE

Equipment: A broom handle or similar object which is approximately three feet in length.

Number of Trials: Two (if necessary)

Directions: Stand close to a wall so that one end of the broom handle can be placed against the flat verticle surface. Hold one end of the handle firmly and place the other end against the wall so that the broom handle extends parallel to the floor. Place the broom handle about level with the child's knee height, the child facing the stick in position for stepping over it (see Fig. 16).

Scoring Criteria: Success if C does not touch broom handle with any part of the body.

Points: Success on first or second trial = 3
Failure on first and second trial = 0

Figure 16. Stepping over a knee-high obstacle.

G-2. DUCKING UNDER A SHOULDER-HIGH OBSTACLE

Equipment: A broom handle or similar object which is approximately
three feet in length.

Number of Trials: Two (if necessary)

Directions: Stand close to a wall so that one end of the broom handle
can be placed against the flat verticle surface. Hold one end
of the handle firmly and place the other end against the wall
so that the broom handle extends parallel to the floor. Place
the broom handle about two inches below the child's shoulder
height so that the child can duck under it (see Fig. 17).

Scoring Criteria: Success if C does not touch broom handle with any
part of the body.

Points: Success on first or second trial = 3
Failure on first and second trial = 0

Figure 17. Ducking under a shoulder-high obstacle.

G-3. PASSING BETWEEN AN OBSTACLE AND A WALL

Equipment: A broom handle or similar object which is approximately
three feet in length.

Number of Trials: Two (if necessary)

Directions: Pull the broom handle away from the wall just far enough so that the C can get between the end of it and the wall if he turns his body sidewise (see Fig. 18).

Scoring Criteria: Success if C does not touch broom handle with any part of the body.

Points: Success on first or second trial $= 3$
Failure on first and second trial $= 0$

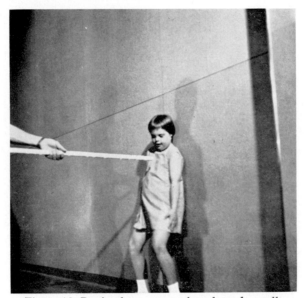

Figure 18. Passing between an obstacle and a wall.

H

H-1. PLACING TEN MATCHSTICKS IN A BOX

Equipment: 4″ × 4″ × 5″ box; ten matchsticks

Number of Trials: One trial with each hand

Directions: Place one row of ten matchsticks approximately one inch apart parallel to the box. The box should be within easy reach of C who is seated at the table so that he can touch the matches with the arm half flexed. C should put matchsticks into the box as fast as he can. He must use only one hand and put in only one matchstick at a time. The matchsticks must be placed and not thrown into the box. E records time to complete the trial. The test is repeated with C using his other hand (see Fig. 19).

Scoring Criteria: The score depends upon the time to complete the task. Maximum time for a trial is sixty seconds. Five seconds

Figure 19. Placing ten matchsticks in a box.

are added to the time score for each error committed. The throwing of matches into the box, or picking up more than one match at a time constitute errors.

Points: 0 - 20 seconds = 3
21 - 40 seconds = 2
41 - 60 seconds = 1
More than 60 seconds = 0

H-2. PLACING TWENTY MATCHSTICKS IN A BOX

Equipment: One 4″ × 4″ × 2″ box and twenty matchsticks
Number of Trials: One
Directions: Box is placed on table within reach of child's hands. Ten matchsticks are placed on either side of box, parallel to each other and about one inch apart. C is to take a matchstick in each hand and place them both in the box at the same time. E records time. (see Fig. 20).
Scoring Criteria: The score depends upon the time to complete the task. Maximum time for a trial is sixty seconds. Five seconds are added to the time score for each error committed. The throwing of matches into the box, picking up more than one

Figure 20. Placing twenty matchsticks in a box.

match at a time in one hand or not picking up a match in each hand at the same time constitute errors.

Points: 0 - 20 seconds = 3
21 - 40 seconds = 2
41 - 60 seconds = 1
More than 60 seconds = 0

H-3. PLACING COINS AND MATCHSTICKS IN BOXES

Equipment: Two 4″ × 4″ × 2″ boxes, ten matchsticks, ten pennies
Number of Trials: One
Directions: The two boxes are placed two inches apart on the table in front of the subject within easy reach of each arm. To the subject's right of the right hand box, ten matchsticks are placed in a row about one inch apart; to the left of the left hand box, ten pennies are placed touching each other in a row. C is to place the pennies in the left hand box and the matches in the right hand box using both hands simultaneously. E records time to complete the task (see Fig. 21).
Scoring Criteria: The score depends upon the time to complete the

Figure 21. Placing coins and matchsticks in boxes.

task. Five seconds are added to the time score for each error committed. Each time C does not place the pieces into the boxes simultaneously, picks up more than one piece at a time, or places the pieces in the wrong box, he is to be corrected verbally by E and five seconds are added to his time score.

Points: 0 - 30 seconds $= 3$
31 - 50 seconds $= 2$
51 - 70 seconds $= 1$
More than 70 seconds $= 0$

I

I-1. WINDING THREAD

Equipment: A spool of thread

Number of Trials: One trial with each hand

Directions: The thread should be allowed to unwind to a distance of two feet and should be fastened securely on one end of the spool. The thread should be unwound when given to C who is seated. C should take the thread between the thumb and index finger of the preferred hand and E should hold the spool at the C's shoulder height. C should wind the thread onto the spool. After the trial with the preferred hand, the task is repeated with the other hand (see Fig. 22).

Scoring Criteria: E notes the exact time C takes to wind the thread. The maximum time limit for a trial is sixty seconds.

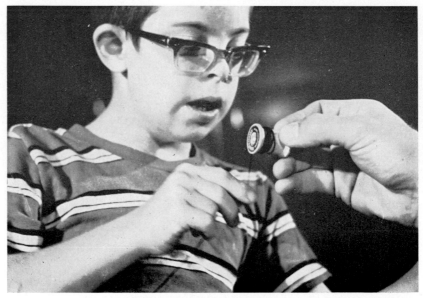

Figure 22. Winding thread.

Points: 0 - 20 seconds = 3
     21 - 40 seconds = 2
     41 - 60 seconds = 1
     More than 60 seconds = 0

I-2. WINDING THREAD WHILE WALKING

Equipment: Spool of thread

Number of Trials: One trial with each hand

Directions: C is to wind a two foot thread around his index finger as quickly as he can while walking. C is given the spool of thread already unwound with the spool attached and dangling at the end. E records time. After the trial with the preferred hand, the test is repeated with C using the other hand (see Fig. 23).

Scoring Criteria: The test is scored according to the time limits given below. If the rhythm of synchronous walking and winding is broken more than five times during the trial, that trial is scored as a complete failure.

Figure 23. Winding thread while walking.

Points: 0 - 21 seconds = 3
         21 - 50 seconds = 2
         51 - 75 seconds = 1
         more than 75 seconds = 0

J

J-1. TAPPING

Equipment: Two sheets of plain paper approximately 8½″ × 11″.
  Lead pencils, with blunt tips.

Number of Trials: One each hand.

Directions: C sits at table with a sheet of plain paper before him. Paper should be fastened to the table so that C can easily reach the paper. At a given signal he is to tap the paper with pencil as rapidly as he can. Dots may be made anywhere on the paper. (see Fig. 24).

Scoring Criteria: Time limit for each trial is twenty seconds. The score for each hand is the number of dots made.

Points: 75 dots and over = 3
  51 - 74 dots = 2
  21 - 50 dots = 1
  20 dots or less = 0

Figure 24. Tapping.

J-2. DRAWING LINES

Equipment: Pencil, a sheet of plain white paper 8½″ × 11″ with
   four pairs of horizontal lines drawn one-half inch apart (see
   Fig. 25).

Number of Trials: Two trials with each hand

Directions: C should be seated at a table with his forearm resting on
   the table and holding the pencil as in a writing position.

   He is to draw as many lines as he can between the two lines.

Scoring Criteria: Time limit, thirty seconds, each hand. The score

Figure 25. Drawing lines.

is the number of lines correctly drawn during the time limit. A line is not counted if it overruns or is short of the horizontal lines on the paper by more than one-fourth of an inch.

Points: 10 lines and over = 3
5 - 9 lines = 2
1 - 4 lines = 1
Less than 1 line = 0

J-3. TRACING MAZES

a. Large Mazes
b. Small Mazes

Equipment: Pencil and mazes
Number of Trials: One trial with each size maze with each hand
Directions: C is seated at the table and is to trace first the large maze with each hand and then the small maze. The entries to the mazes for use with the right hand are in the lower right and the entries for use with the left hand are in the lower left. E should demonstrate the appropriate technique making certain that C understands he is to stay within the boundaries or lines. C may begin by using either his right or left hand, but should complete the large mazes with both hands before attempting the small mazes. E records the time for completion of each maze (see Figs. 26 and 27).

Scoring Criteria: The score for each trial depends upon the amount of time C takes to complete each maze. Five seconds are added to each time score for each error. Going outside the boundary line is an error.

Points:
  a. Large Mazes (each hand)
      0 - 35 seconds = 3
      36 - 50 seconds = 2
      51 - 75 seconds = 1
      Over 75 seconds = 0
  b. Small Mazes (each hand)
      0 - 35 seconds = 3
      36 - 50 seconds = 2
      51 - 75 seconds = 1
      Over 75 seconds = 0

Figure 26. Tracing large mazes.

Figure 27. Tracing small mazes.

K

K-1. CUTTING PAPER WITH SCISSORS

Equipment: Paper strips 8½″ × 3″. Good quality scissors.

Number of Trials: Two trials with each hand

Directions: C is seated at the table and is to cut one strip of paper
into two pieces. C is to cut across the narrow three-inch width
of paper. C may hold the paper in one hand and cut with
the other or may press the paper down on the table to hold
while cutting. E should demonstrate and allow C to practice
cutting with both hands before making the actual trials.

After the trials with one hand, the test should be repeated
with C using his other hand.

Scoring Criteria: Success if C is able to cut completely through the
strip of paper without tearing or pulling it apart.

Points: Success on first or second trial with right hand = 3

Failure on first and second trial with right hand = 0

Success on first or second trial with left hand = 3

Failure on first and second trial with left hand = 0

K-2. CUTTING A STRAIGHT LINE

Equipment: Paper strips 11″ × 6″ with dark line cutting each strip
into two 5¼″ × 6″ boxes (see Fig. 28). Good quality scissors.

Number of Trials: Two trials with each hand

Directions: C is seated at the table and is to cut along the one-half
inch wide dark line for a distance of six inches. C may press
the paper down on the table to hold while cutting. E should
demonstrate and allow C to practice cutting with both hands
before making the actual trials. After the trials with one
hand, the test should be repeated with C using his other hand.

Scoring Criteria: Success if C is able to cut completely through the
strip of paper without tearing or pulling it apart and without
cutting outside the one-half inch dark line.

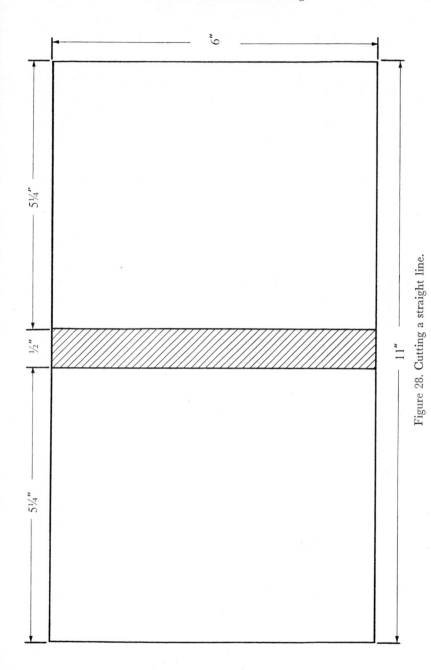

Figure 28. Cutting a straight line.

Points: Success on first or second trial with right hand = 3
Failure on first and second trial with right hand = 0
Success on first or second trial with left hand = 3
Failure on first or second trial with left hand = 0

K-3. CUTTING A CIRCLE

Equipment: Paper with three printed concentric circles with three-fourths inch, 1¼-inch and 1¾-inch radii. Middle circle (1¼″ radius should be darker and wider than other circles (see Fig. 29). Good quality scissors.

Number of Trials: One trial with each hand

Directions: C is to cut a circle into and along the heaviest middle line taking care not to get off the line. E records time. (see Fig. 30).

Scoring Criteria: The score depends upon the time to complete cutting the circle for each hand. Five seconds are added for each

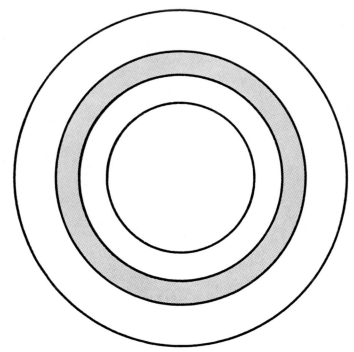

Figure 29. Cutting a circle.

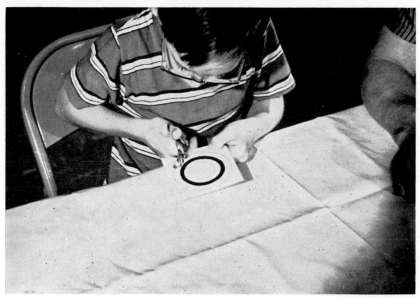

Figure 30. Cutting a circle.

error. An error is counted each time C cuts across the inner or outer circles.

Points for each Hand:

    0 - 30 seconds = 3
    31 - 75 seconds = 2
    76 - 120 seconds = 1
    Over 120 seconds = 0

L

L-1. CATCH TOSSED BALL WITH TWO HANDS

Equipment: Five inch rubber ball.

Number of Trials: Five

Directions: C stands six feet from E with hands cupped and palms facing upward. E lobs the ball to C. If E makes a bad toss, the trial is not counted. (see Fig. 31).

Scoring Criteria: The number of times the ball is caught is recorded. If C makes three successful catches in a row, it is not necessary to make the fourth and fifth throws.

Points: 3 successes = 3

2 successes = 2

1 success = 1

0 success = 0

Figure 31. Catch tossed ball with two hands.

L-2. BOUNCE BALL AND CATCH WITH ONE HAND

Equipment: Five inch rubber ball.

Number of Trials: Five with each hand

Directions: C should bounce the ball once with one hand and catch it with the same hand. One bounce and catch or attempted catch constitutes one trial. Five trials constitute the test for one hand. Following completion of the test for one hand, the test is then repeated with C using the opposite hand.

Scoring Criteria: A success is scored if C is able to throw the ball against the floor and catch it on one bounce with one hand as directed without the aid of the other hand or any other part of the body. The number of times the ball is caught is recorded for each hand. If C makes three successful catches in a row with one hand, it is not necessary to make the fourth and fifth attempts. In the event C uses the wrong hand in catching the ball, E corrects him but does not count the trial.

Points for Each Hand:
  3 successes = 3
  2 successes = 2
  1 success = 1
  0 success = 0

L-3. BOUNCE BALL WITH ONE HAND FIVE TIMES

Equipment: Five inch rubber ball

Number of Trials: Two (if necessary)

Directions: C should keep both feet stationary and bounce ball with one hand five times without catching (see Fig. 32).

Scoring Criteria: Success if C is able to bounce the ball as described at least five times in succession. C may pivot but must not move both feet completely out of position in order to achieve success.

Points: Success on first or second trial = 3
  Failure on both trials = 0

L-4. CATCH TOSSED BALL WITH ONE HAND

Equipment: Five inch rubber ball

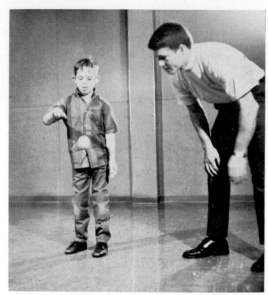

Figure 32. Bounce ball with one hand five times.

Number of Trials: Five with each hand

Directions: C stands six feet from E with one hand behind back and other hand cupped and palm facing upward. E lobs the ball to C. If E makes a bad toss, the trial is not counted. Up to five tosses are made to each hand. (see Fig. 33).

Scoring Criteria: The number of times the ball is caught is recorded for each hand. If C makes three successful catches in a row with the same hand, it is not necessary to make the fourth and fifth throws. In the event C uses the wrong hand in catching the ball, E corrects him but does not count the trial.

Points: 3 successes = 3
2 successes = 2
1 success = 1
0 success = 0

Figure 33. Catch tossed ball with one hand.

M

M-1. THROWING A BALL SIX FEET

Equipment: A six-foot radius circle with a 1' × 1' square outlined in the center. Regulation tennis ball.

Number of Trials: Two with each hand (if necessary)

Directions: C is to stand in the center of the circle and throw the ball through the air in any direction for a distance of six feet. The ball must be thrown in an overhand manner. The foot opposite the hand being used should be placed inside the 1' × 1' square located in the center of the circle. E should demonstrate and allow C to practice several throws with each hand so as to determine if he understands the task. (see Fig. 34).

Scoring Criteria: Success if C stands with one foot inside the center square and correctly throws the ball through the air outside the circle.

Figure 34. Throwing a ball six feet inside a six-foot arc.

Points: Success on first or second trial = 3

Failure on first and second trial = 0

M-2. THROWING A BALL SIX FEET INSIDE A SIX-FOOT ARC

Equipment: A six-foot radius circle with a six-foot arc identified and 1′ × 1′ square in the center of the circle. Regulation tennis ball.

Number of Trials: Two trials with each hand

Directions: C is to stand in the center of the circle and throw the ball through the air for a distance of six feet in the direction of E. The ball should be thrown in an overhand manner. The foot

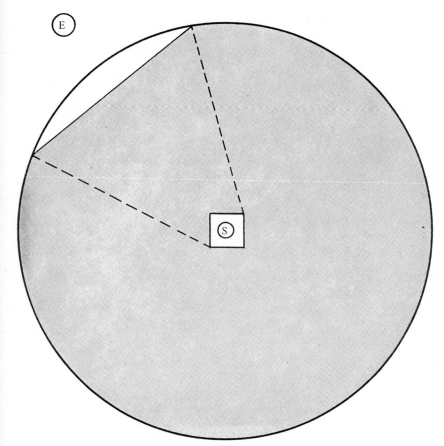

Figure 35. Throwing a ball six feet inside a six-foot arc.

opposite the hand being used should be placed inside the
$1' \times 1'$ square located in the center of the circle. E should
demonstrate so as to show C that he is to throw the ball in
the direction of the identified six-foot arc (see Figs. 34 and
35). C should be allowed to practice several throws with each
hand so as to determine if he understands the task.

Scoring Criteria: Success if C stands with one foot inside the center
square and correctly throws the ball across the specified six-
foot arc marked on the circle.

Points: Success on first or second trial = 3
Failure on first and second trial = 0

M-3. THROWING A BALL AT A TARGET

Equipment: Target ten inches square; regulation tennis ball
Number of Trials: Five trials with each hand
Directions: The target is placed on the wall at a distance of six feet
from front foot of C and at the height of child's chest. The
ball should be thrown in an overhand manner. The opposite
foot should be set forward (see Fig. 36). E should demon-

Figure 36. Throwing a ball at a target.

strate and allow C to practice several throws with each hand before making the trials. Five successive tosses are allowed with one hand and then the test is repeated with C using the other hand.

Scoring Criteria: The score is the number of times the target is hit out of five trials for each hand. If C hits the target three times in a row it is not necessary to make the fourth and fifth throws. If C makes an incorrect throw such as throwing the ball underhand, E corrects him but does not count that trial.

Points: Each hand is scored separately as follows:

3 hits = 3
2 hits = 2
1 hit = 1
0 hits = 0

N

N-1. HANGING FROM PULL-UP BAR

Equipment: Pull-up bar

Number of Trials: One

Directions: C is to stand beneath pull-up bar, grasp bar with palms facing away from body or be lifted so he can grasp bar and be allowed to hang from the bar holding on with two hands with feet off the ground (see Fig. 37).

Scoring Criteria: Success is achieved if C maintains the position for six seconds without dropping from the bar. Points are awarded in accordance with the length of time C hangs from the bar. If C achieves in hanging for thirty seconds, the item is complete.

Figure 37. Hanging from pull-up bar.

[50]

Points: Hanging for:
>   6 - 10 seconds = 1
>   11 - 20 seconds = 2
>   21 - 30 seconds = 3

N-2. PULL-UP TO EYE LEVEL

Equipment: Pull-up bar
Number of Trials: One
Directions: C is to grasp pull-up bar with palms facing away from body and pull his body so that his eyes are level with the bar (see Fig. 38).
Scoring Criteria: C receives one point each time he succeeds in pulling his body to a point where his eyes are level with pull-up bar. C must continue to hang from bar in between pull-ups. Scoring ceases should C drop from bar. Item is complete when C completes three pull-ups.
Points: Score one point for each pull-up with a maximum score of three points.

Figure 38. Pull-up to eye level.

UNIVERSITY OF
ILLINOIS LIBRARY
AT URBANA-CHAMPAIGN

N-3. PULL-UP

Equipment: Pull-up bar

Number of Trials: One

Directions: C is to grasp pull-up bar and pull himself to a position
so that chin is above bar. Hands grasping bar should face
away from body (see Fig. 39).

Scoring Criteria: C receives one point for each time he successfully
raises himself to a position where his chin is at a level
above the bar. C may continue to attempt to complete a valid
pull-up and achieve a score for as long as he is able to hang
on the bar. Once he drops from the bar, the item is completed. If he completes ten pull-ups, the item is also completed.

Points: Score one point for each successful pull-up to a maximum
of ten points.

Figure 39. Pull-up.

O

O-1. LIFT HEAD AND SHOULDERS OFF FLOOR

Equipment: None

Number of Trials: One

Directions: C is to lie on floor with hands clasped behind head and is to raise head and shoulders off the floor (see Fig. 40).

Scoring Criteria: Success if C achieves in lifting head and back to a position just above the buttocks off the floor. Item is completed if C is able to complete three successful lifts off the floor.

Points: Score one point for each successful lift to a maximum of three points.

Figure 40. Lift head and shoulders off floor.

O-2. SIT-UPS

Equipment: None

Number of Trials: One

Directions: C is to lie on floor with fingers clasped behind back of head and is to lift himself to sit-up position. This entails touching one elbow to one knee. Knees may be either bent or in straight position. C may be assisted by having another person hold his ankles (see Fig. 41).

Scoring Criteria: Success is scored if C succeeds in touching his elbow to his knee without unclasping his hands.

Points: Score one point for each successful sit-up to a maximum of ten points.

Figure 41. Sit-ups.

P

P-1. PUSH-UP, HEAD AND SHOULDERS

Equipment: None

Number of Trials: One

Directions: C is to lie face down on the floor with hands directly beneath shoulders. He is to push his head and shoulders from the waist up off the floor, until his arms are straight (see Fig. 42).

Scoring Criteria: Success if C succeeds in pushing head and shoulders from waist off the floor and straightens his arms. Item is complete when C completes three such push-ups.

Points: One point for each successful push-up to a maximum of three points.

Figure 42. Push-up, head and shoulders.

P-2. PUSH-UP FROM KNEES

Equipment: None

Number of Trials: One

Directions: C is to lie face down on the floor with his hands directly beneath his shoulders and push his body from his knees up until his arms are straight (see Fig. 43).

Scoring Criteria: Success if C succeeds in pushing his body from his knees so that he can straighten both arms. Item is completed when C has completed three such push-ups.

Points: Score one point for each successful push-up to a maximum of three points.

Figure 43. Push-up from knees.

P-3. PUSH-UPS

Equipment: None

Number of Trials: One

Directions: C is to lie in a prone position on the floor, face down with hands directly beneath shoulders and push entire body from toes to head until arms are in a straight position. C's body must be in a straight line; it should not sag at the stomach or stick up at the buttocks (see Fig. 44).

Scoring Criteria: Success if C succeeds in pushing his body from the
    floor so that his body maintains a straight line from his toes
    to his head. Item is over when C completes ten such push-ups.

Points: Score one point for each successful push-up to a maximum of
    ten points.

Figure 44. Push-ups.

Q

Q-1. RUNNING FOR A DISTANCE OF FIFTY FEET

Equipment: None

Number of Trials: One

Directions: C is to run in his best manner possible for a distance of fifty feet, perferably in a straight line.

Scoring Criteria: Success if C is able to complete the fifty foot course in twenty seconds or less. If it is necessary for C to change direction across a restricted space, subtract two seconds from C's total time for each turn C is required to make before awarding points.

Points: 1 - 5 seconds = 3
6 - 12 seconds = 2
13 - 20 seconds = 1
over 20 seconds = 0

Q-2. RUN ONE HUNDRED YARDS

Equipment: None

Number of Trials: One

Directions: C is to run for a distance for one hundred yards in his best manner possible, perferably in a straight line.

Scoring Criteria: Success if C is able to complete the one hundred yard course in one hundred seconds or less. If this course has been established in a gymnasium or other large room which require C to reverse his direction, subtract two seconds for each turn which C is required to make before computing score and awarding points.

Points: 1 - 20 seconds = 3
21 - 60 seconds = 2
61 - 100 seconds = 1
Over 100 seconds = 0

Q-3. RUN TWO HUNDRED TWENTY YARDS

Equipment: None

Number of Trials: One

Directions: C is to run for a distance of 220 yards in his best manner possible.

Scoring Criteria: Success if C is able to complete the 220 yard course in three hundred seconds or less.

Points: 1 - 100 seconds = 3
    101 - 200 seconds = 2
    201 - 300 seconds = 1
    over 300 seconds = 0

SCORING SHEET

Name_____ Age_____ Sex_____

Examiner_____ Date_____

Item	Time	Trials	Possible Scores	Points
A.				
1. Standing on tiptoe, eyes open	5 seconds	2	3, 0	
2. Standing on tiptoe, eyes closed	5 seconds	2	3, 0	
3. Crouching on tiptoe	5 seconds	2	3, 0	
B.				
1. Stand heel to toe, eyes open	5 seconds	2	3, 0	
2. Standing heel to toe, eyes closed	5 seconds	2	3, 0	
3. Standing on one foot, eyes open	5 seconds			
Right foot		2	3, 0	
Left foot		2	3, 0	
4. Standing on one foot, eyes closed	5 seconds			
Right foot		2	3, 0	
Left foot		2	3, 0	
C.				
1. Jump on toes rapidly	5 in 5 seconds	2	3, 0	
2. a. Jumping a bar, ankle height		2	3, 0	
b. Jumping a bar, between ankle and knee		2	3, 0	
c. Jumping a bar, knee height		2	3, 0	
D.				
1. Walking forward on stright line of mats		2	3, 0	
2. Walking forward on staggered mats		2	3, 0	
3. Walking forward on a 6' radius semicircle		2	3, 0	
4. Walking forward on a 6' line heel to toe		2	3, 0	
5. Walking backwards—toe to heel, 6 feet		2	3, 0	
E.				
1. Imitations of movements		2	3, 0	
F.				
1. Touching nose (3 times with each hand)		2	3, 0	
2. Touching fingertips				
Right hand		2	3, 0	
Left hand		2	3, 0	
3. Close and open hands alternately	10 seconds	2	3, 0	
4. Tapping rhythmically with feet and fingers	15 seconds	2	3, 0	
G.				
1. Stepping over a knee-high obstacle		2	3, 0	
2. Ducking under a shoulder-high obstacle		2	3, 0	
3. Passing between an obstacle and a wall		2	3, 0	

Item	Time	Trials	Possible Scores	Points
			Seconds Points	
H.				
1. Placing 10 matchsticks in box				
Right hand	0-60 seconds	1	3, 2, 1, 0	
Left hand	0-60 seconds	1	3, 2, 1, 0	
2. Placing 20 matchsticks in a box				
	0-60 seconds	1	3, 2, 1, 0	
3. Placing coins and matchsticks in boxes				
	0-70 seconds	1	3, 2, 1, 0	
I.				
1. Winding thread				
Right hand	0-75 seconds	1	3, 2, 1, 0	
Left hand	0-75 seconds	1	3, 2, 1, 0	
2. Winding thread on finger while walking				
Right hand	0-75 seconds	1	3, 2, 1, 0	
Left hand	0-75 seconds	1	3, 2, 1, 0	
			No. Marks Points	
J.				
1. Tapping				
Right hand	15 seconds	2	3, 2, 1, 0	
Left hand	15 seconds	2	3, 2, 1, 0	
2. Drawing lines				
Right hand	30 seconds	2	3, 2, 1, 0	
Left hand	30 seconds	2	3, 2, 1, 0	
3. Tracing mazes				
a. Large mazes				
Right hand	0-75 seconds	1	3, 2, 1, 0	
Left hand	0-75 seconds	1	3, 2, 1, 0	
b. Small mazes				
Right hand	0-75 seconds	1	3, 2, 1, 0	
Left hand	0-75 seconds	1	3, 2, 1, 0	
K.				*Points*
1. Cutting paper with scissors				
Right hand		2	3, 0	
Left hand		2	3, 0	
2. Cutting a straight line				
Right hand		2	3, 0	
Left hand		2	3, 0	
			Time Points	
3. Cutting a circle				
Right hand	0-120 seconds	1	3, 2, 1, 0	
Left hand	0-120 seconds	1	3, 2, 1, 0	
L.			*Successes Points*	
1. Catch tossed ball with two hands		5	3, 2, 1, 0	
2. Bounce ball and catch with one hand				
Right hand		5	3, 2, 1, 0	
Left hand		5	3, 2, 1, 0	
			Points	
3. Bounce ball with one hand five times				
Right hand		2	3, 0	
Left hand		2	3, 0	
4. Catch tossed ball with one hand			*Successes Points*	
Right hand		5	3, 2, 1, 0	
Left hand		5	3, 2, 1, 0	

Item	Time	Trials	Possible Scores	Points
M.				
1. Throwing a ball, 6 feet				
Right hand		2	3, 0	
Left hand		2	3, 0	
2. Throwing a ball 6 feet inside a 6 foot arc				
Right hand		2	3, 0	
Left hand		2	3, 0	
3. Throwing a ball at a target			*Hits*	*Points*
Right hand		5	3, 2, 1, 0	
Left hand		5	3, 2, 1, 0	
N.			*Seconds*	*Points*
1. Hanging from pull-up bar	0-30 seconds	1	3, 2, 1, 0	
				Points
2. Pull-up to eye level		1	3, 2, 1, 0	
3. Pull-up		1	10, 9, 8, 7, 6, 5, 4, 3, 2, 1, 0	
O.				
1. Lift head and shoulders off floor		1	3, 2, 1, 0	
2. Sit-up		1	10, 9, 8, 7, 6, 5, 4, 3, 2, 1, 0	
P.				
1. Push-up, head and shoulders		1	3, 2, 1, 0	
2. Push-up from knees		1	3, 2, 1, 0	
3. Push-up		1	10, 9, 8, 7, 6, 5, 4, 3, 2, 1, 0	
Q.				
1. Running, 50 feet	0-20 seconds	1	3, 2, 1, 0	
2. Running, 100 yards	0-100 seconds	1	3, 2, 1, 0	
3. Running, 220 yards	0-300 seconds	1	3, 2, 1, 0	

INDEX